Pebble Plus

Animal Offspring

Cows and Their Calves

Revised Edition

Margaret Hall

Raintree is an imprint of Capstone Global Library Limited, a company incorporated in England and Wales having its registered office at 264 Banbury Road, Oxford, OX2 7DY – Registered company number: 6695582

www.raintree.co.uk
myorders@raintree.co.uk

ISBN 978 1 4747 5625 9 (hardback)
22 21 20 19 18
10 9 8 7 6 5 4 3 2 1

ISBN 978 1 4747 5635 8 (paperback)
23 22 21 20 19
10 9 8 7 6 5 4 3 2 1

British Library Cataloging in Publication Data
A full catalogue record for this book is available from the British Library.

Editorial Credits
Gina Kammer, editor; Sarah Bennett, designer; Morgan Walters, media researcher; Katy LaVigne, production specialist

Printed and bound in India

Acknowledgements
We would like to thank the following for permission to reproduce photographs: Shutterstock: alberto clemares exposito, 19, arogant, right 20, Barsan ATTILA, 13, Ewelina Wachala, right 21, GLF Media, 5, Ilia Krivoruk, 9, ivan jimenez foto, 7, jennyt, Cover, jungdosoon, 1, Lakeview Images, 11, MRAORAOR, 15, napocska, left 20, Nicole Kwiatkowski, 17, Rosa Jay, left 21

Every effort has been made to contact copyright holders of material reproduced in this book. Any omissions will be rectified in subsequent printings if notice is given to the publisher.

All the Internet addresses (URLs) given in this book were valid at the time of going to press. However, due to the dynamic nature of the Internet, some addresses may have changed, or sites may have changed or ceased to exist since publication. While the author and publisher regret any inconvenience this may cause readers, no responsibility for any such changes can be accepted by either the author or the publisher.

Contents

Cows

Cows are mammals.

Cows have black, brown,

white or red hair.

Young cows are

called calves.

5

Cows and calves graze
in fields on farms. Cows and
calves sometimes live
in barns.

A male is a bull.

A female is a cow.

Bulls and cows mate.

A calf begins to grow

inside the cow.

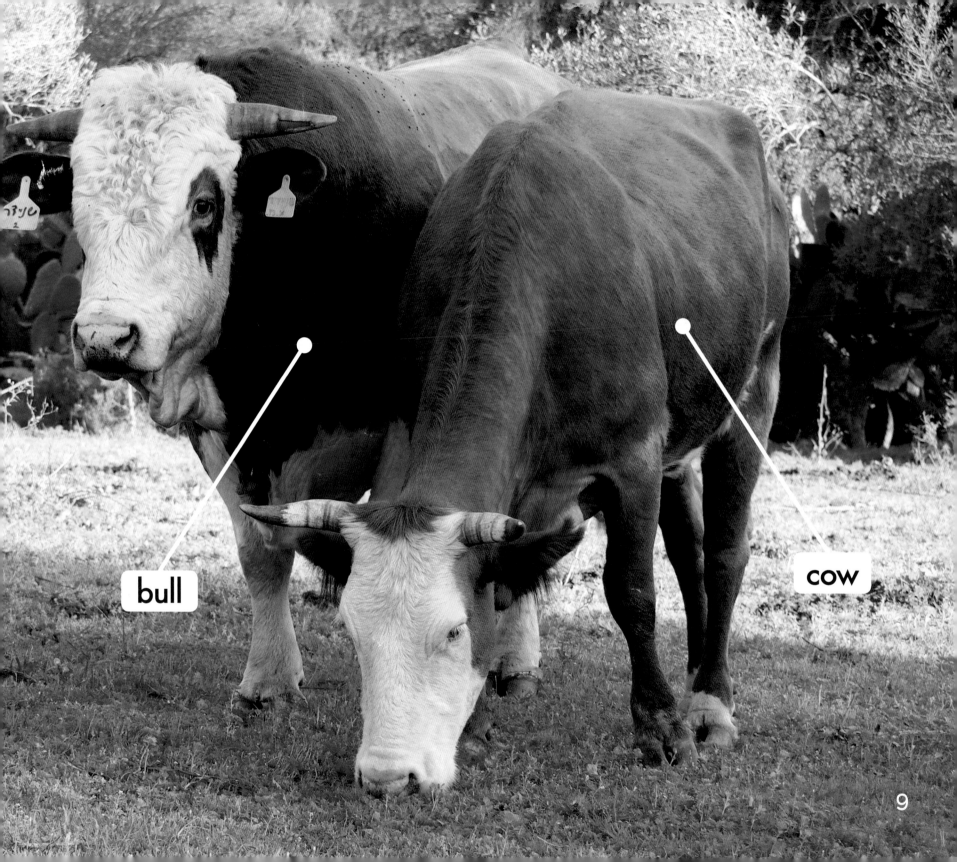

bull

cow

The calf

The cow gives birth
to a calf.
The cow takes care
of the calf.

Calves have long legs.

Calves can stand up about one

hour after they are born.

Calves drink milk

from their mothers.

Growing up

Calves start to eat
hay, grass and grain
after about one month.

Calves become adults
after about two years.

Watch cows grow

birth

adult after
about two years

Glossary

birth event of being born; cows usually give birth to one calf at a time; cows sometimes have twins

bull adult male of the cattle family; bulls can father young; male calves that do not become fathers are called steers

cow adult female of the cattle family; a young cow is called a heifer before she gives birth to a calf for the first time

graze eat grass and other plants that are growing in a pasture or field

mammal warm–blooded animal that has a backbone and hair or fur; female mammals feed milk to their young

mate join together to produce young; cows give birth nine months after mating

Find out more

Books

Animals on the Farm (Animals I can See), Sian Smith (Raintree, 2015)

Calves (Farm Babies), Tim Mayerling (Tadpole Books, 2017)

Mammal Babies (Animal Babies), Catherine Veitch (Raintree, 2014)

Websites

www.activityvillage.co.uk/cows
Activity Village

www.bbc.co.uk/cbeebies/games/down-on-the-farm-a-year-on-your-farm
BBC

Comprehension questions

1. What things can a calf do soon after it is born?

2. Cows and calves graze in fields. What does "graze" mean?

3. How does a cow take care of her calf?

Index